LLC BEGINNERS

GUIDE

2024 - 2025

A Complete Step-By-Step Handbook On How To Form, Manage & Maintain Your Limited Liability Company

Mike R. Peterson

<u>Dedication</u>

To the relentless spirit of entrepreneurship, this book is dedicated to aspiring business leaders who embark on the transformative journey of creating and nurturing their Limited Liability Companies (LLCs).

It is a tribute to the innovators, risk-takers, and visionaries who dare to turn dreams into enterprises. To those who navigate the complexities of business ownership with resilience, determination, and a thirst for knowledge, this guide is crafted for you.

May the insights within these pages empower you to make informed decisions, overcome challenges, and achieve enduring success in the dynamic realm of entrepreneurship. This book is dedicated to the entrepreneurs who shape the future, one LLC at a time.

<u>Appreciation</u>

As we start this journey through the intricacies of Limited Liability Companies (LLCs), I extend heartfelt gratitude to you, the reader. Your pursuit of knowledge and commitment to entrepreneurial excellence inspire me.

The success of this guide lies in your curiosity, determination, and passion for building and growing businesses. I hope the insights provided will enrich your understanding and equip you for success in your ventures. Your journey is our shared venture, and your feedback is invaluable.

I invite you to leave a review, sharing your thoughts and experiences. May your LLC thrive, and your entrepreneurial spirit continue to shape a future of innovation and prosperity. Thank you for being an integral part of this entrepreneurial community.

Table Of Contents

Chapter 1

Understanding the Basics of LLCs

Limited Liability Companies (LLCs) have become a popular choice for entrepreneurs seeking a flexible and protective business structure. In this chapter, we will delve into the foundational aspects of LLCs, exploring their introduction, advantages, disadvantages, and key features.

1.1 Introduction to Limited Liability Companies

Limited Liability Companies, or LLCs, represent a hybrid business structure that combines the liability protection of a corporation with the simplicity and flexibility of a partnership. Established as a legal entity separate from its owners, or members, an LLC provides a level of personal asset protection that is crucial for entrepreneurs navigating the complexities of the business world.

The concept of an LLC emerged to address the limitations and rigidities associated with traditional business structures. It offers a middle ground between sole proprietorships or partnerships, where personal assets are at risk, and corporations, which can be administratively burdensome.

One of the defining features of an LLC is its flexibility in management and organization. Unlike corporations with a strict hierarchy and governance structure, LLCs allow members to determine how the company will be managed. This adaptability makes them an attractive option for small and medium-sized businesses, as well as startups, seeking a customizable and scalable structure.

1.2 Advantages and Disadvantages of LLCs

Understanding the advantages and disadvantages of forming an LLC is crucial for any entrepreneur considering this business structure. Let's explore both sides of the coin to make an informed decision.

Advantages:

1. **Limited Liability:** As the name suggests, one of the primary advantages of an LLC is the limited liability protection it offers to its members. This means that personal assets of the members are generally protected from business debts and liabilities. In the event of legal action or financial difficulties, the members' personal assets are shielded.

2. **Flexibility in Management:** Unlike corporations, which have a more rigid management structure, LLCs allow for flexibility in decision-making. Members can choose a management structure that suits the needs and dynamics of their business.

3. **Pass-Through Taxation:** LLCs benefit from pass-through taxation, meaning that profits and losses "pass through" the business to the individual members. This avoids the double taxation that corporations may face, enhancing the overall tax efficiency of the LLC.

4. **Simplified Compliance:** LLCs generally have fewer compliance requirements compared to corporations. There is often less paperwork

and regulatory burden, making it an attractive option for small business owners.

Disadvantages:

1. **Limited Capital Raising Options:** Unlike corporations, which can issue stocks to raise capital, LLCs may face limitations in attracting investment. This can be a drawback for businesses with ambitious growth plans.

2. **Potential Complexity in Management:** While flexibility is a strength, it can also be a challenge. The lack of a standardized management structure may lead to complications, especially if there are disagreements among members regarding decision-making.

3. **State Variability:** The laws governing LLCs can vary from state to state. Entrepreneurs need to navigate the specific regulations of the state in which they choose to establish their LLC, potentially adding complexity to the formation process.

4. **Perceived Lack of Prestige:** In certain industries or regions, there may be a perception that corporations carry more prestige than LLCs. This could potentially impact relationships with clients, customers, or investors.

1.3 Key Features and Characteristics

To fully grasp the dynamics of LLCs, it is essential to delve into their key features and characteristics that set them apart in the business landscape.

1. **Limited Liability:** Perhaps the most fundamental feature of an LLC is the protection it offers to its members. The personal assets of members are typically shielded from business debts and legal liabilities, reducing the risk associated with entrepreneurship.

2. **Flexible Management Structure:** LLCs provide a versatile approach to management. Members can choose between a member-managed structure, where all members are actively involved in decision-making, or a manager-managed structure, where designated individuals handle day-to-day operations.

3. **Pass-Through Taxation:** The pass-through taxation characteristic means that the profits and losses of the LLC are passed through to the individual members. This avoids the double taxation that corporations may face and allows for a more straightforward tax structure.

4. **Operating Agreement:** While not always a legal requirement, an operating agreement is a crucial document for LLCs. This internal document outlines the structure and operation of the business, including the roles and responsibilities of members, management processes, and dispute resolution mechanisms.

5. **Ease of Formation:** Compared to corporations, LLCs are relatively easy to form. The process involves filing articles of organization with the appropriate state authority, specifying key details such as the business name, address, and members.

6. **Ownership Flexibility:** LLCs can have a flexible ownership structure. Members can include individuals, other LLCs, corporations,

or even foreign entities. This adaptability allows for a diverse range of ownership scenarios.

Understanding these key features and characteristics lays the groundwork for entrepreneurs to make informed decisions when considering an LLC as their preferred business structure. The balance between advantages and disadvantages, coupled with the flexibility inherent in LLCs, makes them an appealing choice for a wide range of business ventures.

In conclusion, Chapter 1 has provided a comprehensive overview of Limited Liability Companies, offering a glimpse into their introduction, the advantages and disadvantages they present, and the key features that define their structure. Armed with this knowledge, entrepreneurs can proceed to Chapter 2, where we will explore the critical decision-making process of determining if an LLC is the right fit for their unique business endeavors.

Chapter 2

Deciding if an LLC is Right for You

As an entrepreneur embarks on the journey of establishing a business, one of the pivotal decisions is choosing the most suitable business structure. In this chapter, we will delve into the intricate process of determining if a Limited Liability Company (LLC) aligns with the unique characteristics and goals of your venture. We'll explore the advantages and potential drawbacks of an LLC and compare it to other business structures to guide you in making an informed decision.

2.1 Is an LLC the Right Business Structure for Your Venture?

The decision to structure your business as an LLC requires a thoughtful analysis of various factors that influence the overall success and sustainability of your venture. Let's explore key considerations to help you determine if an LLC is the right fit for your business.

Business Nature and Size:

Consider the nature and size of your business. LLCs are well-suited for small to medium-sized enterprises, offering flexibility in management and a streamlined organizational structure. If your business is relatively small and you desire a simplified operational framework, an LLC may align with your vision.

Liability Protection:

Evaluate the level of liability protection your business requires. If your venture involves inherent risks, such as providing professional services or dealing with potential legal disputes, an LLC's limited liability feature can be a significant advantage. It shields your personal assets from business debts and legal liabilities, providing a crucial layer of protection.

Tax Considerations:

Examine your preferences regarding taxation. LLCs benefit from pass-through taxation, meaning that profits and losses are passed through to individual members. This can be advantageous, especially if you want to avoid the double taxation associated with corporations. If you seek a straightforward tax structure with flexibility in allocating profits, an LLC may be the right choice.

Management Structure:

Consider your preferred management style. LLCs offer flexibility in management, allowing members to choose between a member-managed or manager-managed structure. If you prefer active involvement in decision-making or want to designate specific individuals for management roles, the adaptable management structure of an LLC can align with your preferences.

Future Growth and Funding:

Contemplate your long-term business goals. If you envision significant growth and plan to attract external investments through issuing stocks, a corporation might be a more suitable choice. While LLCs offer advantages, they may have limitations in raising capital through traditional means.

State Regulations:

Be aware of state-specific regulations. LLC laws can vary from state to state, impacting factors such as formation requirements, reporting obligations, and member rights. Research the regulations in the state where you plan to establish your LLC to ensure compliance with local laws.

Operational Simplicity:
Assess your desire for operational simplicity. If you prefer a business structure with fewer formalities and administrative requirements, an LLC might be a favorable option. Corporations often involve more complex governance structures and compliance obligations.

By carefully analyzing these factors, you can gain clarity on whether an LLC aligns with the unique characteristics and goals of your venture. Remember that the decision-making process is not one-size-fits-all, and what works for one business may not be suitable for another. It's essential to tailor your choice of business structure to the specific needs and aspirations of your enterprise.

2.2 Comparing LLCs to Other Business Structures

To make an informed decision about structuring your business, it's crucial to compare LLCs with other common business structures. Let's explore the distinctions between LLCs, sole proprietorships, partnerships, and corporations, shedding light on the unique features of each.

Sole Proprietorship:
A sole proprietorship is the simplest form of business structure, where a single individual owns and operates the business. While easy to set up and manage, sole proprietorships lack the liability protection afforded by an LLC. The owner is personally responsible for all business debts and legal obligations. If simplicity is a priority and your business is of modest scale with minimal risk, a sole proprietorship may be a viable option.

Partnership:
Partnerships involve two or more individuals sharing ownership and management

responsibilities. Like sole proprietorships, partnerships lack the limited liability protection of an LLC. General partnerships expose each partner to personal liability for the business's debts and actions. If you are considering a partnership, it's crucial to establish a clear partnership agreement outlining roles, responsibilities, and profit-sharing to mitigate potential conflicts.

Corporation:

Corporations, both C corporations and S corporations, are distinct legal entities with shareholders, directors, and officers. One primary advantage of corporations is their ability to issue stocks, facilitating capital raising. However, corporations also face double taxation, where the business itself is taxed on profits, and shareholders are taxed on dividends. If you anticipate significant growth and plan to go public or attract substantial investments, a corporation may be the preferred choice.

Limited Liability Partnership (LLP):

An LLP is a hybrid structure that combines elements of partnerships and corporations. While it provides some level of liability protection, it may not be as comprehensive as an LLC. LLPs are often chosen by professional service providers, such as law or accounting firms. If you seek a middle ground between a partnership and an LLC, an LLP could be a suitable alternative.

Choosing Between LLCs and Other Structures:

The decision between an LLC and other structures hinges on factors such as liability protection, taxation preferences, management style, and growth aspirations. Here are key points to consider when comparing LLCs to other business structures:

- **Liability Protection**: If limited liability is a priority, an LLC or a corporation is preferable over sole proprietorships or partnerships.

- **Taxation**: If pass-through taxation is essential, LLCs are advantageous compared to C corporations. S corporations also offer pass-through taxation but come with specific eligibility criteria.

- **Management Flexibility:** For entrepreneurs who value flexibility in management and decision-making, LLCs provide more adaptability compared to corporations with stricter governance structures.

- **Capital Raising:** If your business plans involve substantial capital raising through issuing stocks, a corporation might be the most suitable option.

- **Operational Simplicity:** If you prioritize a streamlined operational structure with fewer formalities, LLCs are generally simpler compared to corporations.

In making this critical decision, it is advisable to seek professional advice from legal and financial experts who can provide tailored guidance based on your business's unique circumstances. Additionally, staying informed about the specific regulations and requirements in your state is crucial to ensuring compliance with local laws.

As you navigate the comparison between LLCs and other business structures, keep in mind that each has its strengths and weaknesses. The optimal choice depends on your business goals, risk tolerance, and preferences. This careful evaluation sets the foundation for a business structure that aligns seamlessly with your entrepreneurial vision.

Chapter 3

Step-by-Step Guide to Forming an LLC

Forming a Limited Liability Company (LLC) is a pivotal step in establishing a business with legal recognition and protection. In this chapter, we will provide a comprehensive step-by-step guide to help you navigate the process of forming an LLC. From choosing a name and checking its availability to preparing and filing the Articles of Organization, and finally, creating an Operating Agreement, each step is crucial for a seamless and legally sound formation.

3.1 Naming Your LLC and Checking Availability

Choosing the right name for your LLC is more than just a creative endeavor; it's a strategic decision with legal implications. The name you select will represent your business, distinguish it from others, and contribute to its brand identity. Here's a detailed guide to the first step of forming an LLC – naming and checking the availability of your chosen name.

Selecting a Unique and Distinctive Name:

1. **Reflect Your Business Identity:** Choose a name that reflects the nature of your business and resonates with your target audience. Consider the values, products, or services that set your business apart.

2. **Consider Future Growth:** Think long-term. Select a name that accommodates potential expansion or diversification of your business. Avoid overly narrow names that may limit your company's evolution.

3. **Check Legal Requirements:** Ensure that your chosen name complies with legal requirements in your state. Some states may have specific rules regarding words that must be included (e.g., "Limited Liability Company" or its abbreviation).

Checking Name Availability:

1. **State Business Registry:** Begin by checking the availability of your chosen name in the state's business registry. Most states have online databases where you can search for existing business names. Ensure that no other LLC or business entity is already using a similar or identical name.

2. **Domain Availability**: In today's digital age, securing a matching domain is crucial for an online presence. Check the availability of your desired domain to ensure consistency across your business's online and offline identity.

3. **Trademark Search**: Conduct a thorough trademark search to ensure that your chosen name is not already trademarked by another entity. This step is essential for avoiding potential legal conflicts and protecting your brand.

4. **Reserved Name Option:** Some states allow you to reserve a business name for a specific period before officially registering your LLC. If you need time to complete other aspects of the

formation process, consider taking advantage of this option.

Additional Considerations:

1. **Avoid Misleading Names:** Ensure that your chosen name does not mislead the public about the nature of your business. Avoid names that may imply governmental affiliations or use prohibited terms.

2. **Check Social Media Handles:** Verify the availability of your chosen name on major social media platforms. Consistency across various online channels contributes to a cohesive brand image.

Once you have chosen a unique and available name for your LLC, you can proceed to the next crucial step in the formation process.

3.2 Preparing and Filing Articles of Organization

The Articles of Organization, also known as the Certificate of Formation or Certificate of Organization in some states, is a fundamental document required to officially register your

LLC with the state. This document provides essential information about your business and its structure. Let's break down the process of preparing and filing the Articles of Organization.

Information to Include in the Articles of Organization:

1. **Business Name and Address**: Clearly state the legal name of your LLC, ensuring it matches the name you've selected and checked for availability. Provide the physical address of your business, which can be a physical location or a registered agent's address.

2. **Registered Agent:** Designate a registered agent for your LLC. A registered agent is a person or entity responsible for receiving legal documents, such as lawsuits or official correspondence, on behalf of the LLC. Ensure that the registered agent has a physical address in the state where you are forming the LLC.

3. **Business Purpose:** Describe the purpose or nature of your business. This can be a general statement, such as "to engage in any lawful

business activity," or a specific description of the products or services your business will provide.

4. **Management Structure:** Indicate whether your LLC will be member-managed or manager-managed. In a member-managed LLC, all members participate in decision-making, while in a manager-managed LLC, designated individuals (managers) handle day-to-day operations.

5. **Member Information:** Provide the names and addresses of the initial members of the LLC. Some states may also require information about the percentage of ownership each member holds.

6. **Duration of the LLC:** Specify whether your LLC is formed for a specific period (limited duration) or whether it is intended to exist indefinitely (perpetual duration).

Filing the Articles of Organization:

1. **Access State Filing Forms:** Obtain the official Articles of Organization form from the

website of the state's business or corporate filing office. Most states provide downloadable forms with instructions.

2. **Complete the Form:** Fill out the form accurately and completely. Double-check all information, ensuring accuracy in names, addresses, and other details.

3. **Filing Fee:** Pay the required filing fee along with the submission of the Articles of Organization. The fee amount varies by state and is typically payable by check or online payment.

4. **Submit the Form:** Submit the completed form and payment to the appropriate state office. This is often the Secretary of State's office or a similar agency responsible for business registrations.

Wait for Approval:

1. **Processing Time**: The processing time for approving the Articles of Organization varies by state. Some states offer expedited processing for an additional fee.

2. **Confirmation of Approval:** Once approved, you will receive confirmation, and your LLC will be officially registered with the state. This confirmation may include a stamped copy of the filed Articles of Organization.

Post-Approval Steps:

1. **Obtain EIN:** After receiving approval, obtain an Employer Identification Number (EIN) from the IRS. An EIN is necessary for various purposes, including opening a business bank account and filing taxes.

2. **Compliance with Additional Requirements:** Some states may have additional requirements or ongoing compliance obligations for LLCs. Familiarize yourself with these and ensure ongoing compliance with state regulations.

By following these steps, you will successfully complete the process of preparing and filing the Articles of Organization, marking a significant milestone in the formalization of your LLC.

3.3 Creating an Operating Agreement

While not always a legal requirement, creating an Operating Agreement is a highly recommended step in forming an LLC. This internal document outlines the structure and operation of your business, defining the roles and responsibilities of members, management processes, and other crucial details. Let's explore the importance of an Operating Agreement and the key elements to include.

Importance of an Operating Agreement:

1. **Clarity in Member Roles:** An Operating Agreement clarifies the roles and responsibilities of each member. It outlines the decision-making processes, management responsibilities, and the level of involvement each member has in the day-to-day operations.

2. **Dispute Resolution:** In the event of disagreements or disputes among members, an Operating Agreement provides a framework for resolution. Clearly defined dispute resolution mechanisms can help prevent conflicts from escalating and damaging the business.

3. **Distribution of Profits and Losses**: The Operating Agreement establishes how profits and losses will be distributed among members. This flexibility allows for customized allocation based on the contributions and agreements among members.

4. **Ownership and Transfer of Membership Interests:** Clearly outline the ownership structure of the LLC and any restrictions on the transfer of membership interests. This is crucial for maintaining control over the composition of the LLC.

5. **Admission of New Members**: If the possibility of admitting new members exists, the Operating Agreement should specify the process for doing so. This ensures transparency and a smooth transition when bringing in new stakeholders.

6. **Dissolution Procedures:** In the unfortunate event that the LLC needs to be dissolved, the Operating Agreement provides guidelines for the process. This includes how assets will be distributed, debts settled, and the steps involved in formally dissolving the business.

Key Elements to Include in the Operating Agreement:

1. **Business Name and Purpose**: Begin with the basics, stating the legal name and purpose of the LLC as outlined in the Articles of Organization.

2. **Members' Contributions**: Clearly detail the contributions made by each member, whether in the form of capital, assets, or services. This section establishes the initial equity and contributions of each member.

3. **Distribution of Profits and Losses**: Outline the criteria for distributing profits and losses among members. This can be based on ownership percentages or other agreed-upon criteria.

4. **Management Structure:** Specify whether the LLC is member-managed or manager-managed. If it is manager-managed, provide details about the designated managers and their roles.

5. **Decision-Making Processes**: Define the decision-making processes, including voting rights and procedures for major business decisions. Clearly outline which decisions require unanimous consent and which can be made by a majority.

6. **Transfer of Membership Interests**: If members are allowed to transfer their ownership interests, detail the process and any restrictions or conditions associated with such transfers.

7. **Dispute Resolution:** Establish mechanisms for resolving disputes among members. This can include mediation, arbitration, or other agreed-upon methods to avoid costly and time-consuming legal battles.

8. **Dissolution Procedures:** Clearly articulate the procedures for dissolving the LLC, including how assets will be distributed and debts settled. This section is essential for providing a roadmap in case the business needs to wind down.

Legal Review and Professional Assistance:

1. **Legal Review:** While Operating Agreements are often flexible and customizable, it's advisable to have the document reviewed by legal professionals to ensure compliance with state laws and regulations.

2. **Professional Assistance**: If needed, seek the assistance of legal and financial professionals to help draft or review the Operating Agreement. Their expertise can provide valuable insights and ensure that all relevant aspects are addressed.

Updating the Operating Agreement:

1. **Periodic Review:** Regularly review and update the Operating Agreement to reflect any changes in the business structure, membership, or operating processes. This ensures that the document remains relevant and effective over time.

2. **Member Consensus:** Any updates to the Operating Agreement should be made with the consensus of all members. This collaborative approach helps maintain a positive and transparent business environment.

In conclusion, creating an Operating Agreement is a critical step in formalizing the structure and operation of your LLC. This internal document provides a solid foundation for the smooth functioning of the business and serves as a reference point for members in various scenarios.

By combining legal requirements with thoughtful customization, you can create an Operating Agreement that aligns with the unique needs and aspirations of your LLC. With the completion of this step, your LLC is now well-positioned for success, equipped with a clear roadmap for its operation and governance.

Chapter 4

Legal and Regulatory Compliance for LLCs

Ensuring legal and regulatory compliance is an integral aspect of managing a successful Limited Liability Company (LLC). In this chapter, we will delve into the complexities of legal and regulatory requirements for LLCs, covering crucial areas such as taxation, compliance with state and federal regulations, and the importance of annual reporting and record-keeping.

4.1 Understanding Taxation for LLCs

Taxation is a key consideration for any business entity, and understanding the tax implications of an LLC is paramount for both operational efficiency and financial planning. LLCs benefit from a unique tax structure known as pass-through taxation. Let's explore this and other important aspects related to taxation for LLCs.

Pass-Through Taxation:

1. Flow-Through of Profits and Losses: One of the primary advantages of an LLC is pass-through taxation. This means that the profits and losses of the LLC "pass through" to the individual members, who report these on their personal income tax returns. This avoids the double taxation that corporations may face, where the business itself is taxed on its profits, and shareholders are taxed on dividends.

2. Flexibility in Profit Allocation: LLCs have flexibility in allocating profits among members. This can be based on ownership percentages or structured according to specific agreements among members. The ability to customize profit allocations allows for strategic tax planning based on the financial goals and preferences of the members.

Classification for Federal Tax Purposes:

1. Default Classification: By default, an LLC with multiple members is classified as a partnership for federal tax purposes. This means that it follows the pass-through taxation model.

2. **Single-Member LLC:** If an LLC has only one member, it is treated as a "disregarded entity" for federal tax purposes. The IRS disregards the LLC, and the member reports the business income and expenses on their personal tax return.

3. **Electing Corporate Taxation:** In certain situations, an LLC may choose to be taxed as a corporation. This election is made by filing Form 8832 with the IRS. However, this decision should be made carefully, considering the specific tax implications for the business and its members.

Self-Employment Taxes and Social Security:

1. **Self-Employment Taxes**: Members of an LLC are generally considered self-employed and are subject to self-employment taxes. This includes contributions to Social Security and Medicare.

2. **Social Security and Medicare Contributions**: Members must pay both the employer and employee portions of Social

Security and Medicare taxes. This is an important consideration for members managing their personal finances and planning for future retirement benefits.

State Tax Obligations:

1. **State Income Taxes:** LLCs are subject to state income taxes, and the specific requirements vary by state. Some states may impose an annual tax on the LLC's income or require additional filings.

2. **Franchise Taxes:** Some states levy franchise taxes on LLCs, which are separate from income taxes. It's crucial to be aware of and fulfill these obligations to maintain good standing with the state.

Tax Planning Considerations:

1. **Consultation with Tax Professionals:** Given the complexity of tax regulations, it is advisable for LLCs to seek the guidance of tax professionals. They can provide insights into strategic tax planning, deductions, and credits that may benefit the business and its members.

2. **Estimated Tax Payments:** Members of an LLC may be required to make estimated tax payments throughout the year. This helps avoid penalties for underpayment of taxes and ensures compliance with tax obligations.

3. **Record-Keeping for Deductions:** Maintaining accurate and detailed records is crucial for claiming deductions and credits. This includes records of business expenses, income, and any relevant financial transactions.

Understanding the taxation landscape for LLCs is a foundational aspect of legal compliance. By navigating these considerations diligently and seeking professional advice when needed, LLCs can optimize their tax structure to support financial goals and maintain compliance with federal and state tax regulations.

4.2 Compliance with State and Federal Regulations

Compliance with state and federal regulations is a fundamental responsibility for LLCs. Staying abreast of legal requirements is essential to avoid legal issues, financial penalties, and potential disruptions to business operations. Let's explore key aspects of compliance with both state and federal regulations for LLCs.

State Regulations:

1. **Articles of Organization**: The initial step in compliance is the proper filing of the Articles of Organization with the state. This document officially registers the LLC and provides essential information about its structure and purpose.

2. **Registered Agent:** LLCs are required to have a registered agent with a physical address in the state of formation. The registered agent is responsible for receiving legal documents and official correspondence on behalf of the LLC.

3. **Annual Reports:** Many states require LLCs to file annual reports, providing updated information about the business, its members, and its activities. These reports may include details such as changes in membership, business address, and other relevant information.

4. Business Licenses and Permits: LLCs must obtain any necessary business licenses and permits to operate legally within a state. Requirements vary by location and industry, so it's crucial to research and comply with local regulations.

5. State Tax Obligations: In addition to federal taxes, LLCs are subject to state taxes. This includes income taxes and any applicable state-specific taxes. Compliance with state tax obligations is essential for maintaining good standing with the state.

6. Employee Regulations: If the LLC has employees, compliance with state labor laws is paramount. This includes adhering to minimum wage requirements, employee classifications, and workplace safety regulations.

Federal Regulations:

1. Employer Identification Number (EIN): Obtaining an EIN from the IRS is a federal requirement for LLCs. This unique identifier is necessary for various purposes, including opening a business bank account, hiring employees, and filing federal taxes.

2. **Employee Taxes:** LLCs with employees must comply with federal employment tax obligations. This includes withholding and remitting income taxes, Social Security, and Medicare taxes from employee wages.

3. **Independent Contractor Compliance:** If the LLC engages independent contractors, it must ensure compliance with IRS guidelines for proper classification. Misclassifying workers can lead to legal and financial consequences.

4. **Federal Tax Filings:** LLCs with more than one member are generally treated as partnerships for federal tax purposes and must file Form 1065, U.S. Return of Partnership Income. Single-member LLCs report business income and expenses on the owner's personal tax return.

5. **Compliance with Federal Securities Laws:** If an LLC plans to raise capital through the sale of securities, compliance with federal securities laws is essential. This includes adherence to

regulations set forth by the Securities and Exchange Commission (SEC).

Ongoing Compliance Practices:

1. **Regular Audits and Assessments:** Regularly audit the business's practices to ensure ongoing compliance with state and federal regulations. This includes reviewing changes in regulations that may impact the business.

2. **Employee Handbook and Policies:** Establishing and maintaining an employee handbook with clearly defined policies ensures compliance with employment laws and provides a framework for employee conduct.

3. **Training for Compliance:** Educate employees on relevant compliance requirements. This may include training on workplace safety, discrimination and harassment prevention, and other regulatory matters.

4. **Record-Keeping:** Maintain comprehensive records of business activities, financial

transactions, and compliance efforts. Detailed records serve as evidence of compliance in the event of an audit or legal inquiry.

5. **Legal Consultation**: Seek legal advice when faced with complex compliance issues. Legal professionals can provide guidance on specific regulations and help navigate intricate legal matters.

Compliance with state and federal regulations is an ongoing commitment that requires diligence and proactive measures. By integrating compliance practices into the day-to-day operations of an LLC, businesses can build a solid foundation for sustained growth and success.

4.3 Annual Reporting and Record-Keeping

Annual reporting and record-keeping are critical components of maintaining an LLC's good standing and legal compliance. These practices not only fulfill legal requirements but also contribute to effective business management and decision-making. Let's explore the importance of annual reporting and record-keeping for LLCs.

Annual Reporting:

1. **Fulfilling State Requirements**: Many states require LLCs to file annual reports, also known as annual statements or annual renewals. These reports provide updated information about the LLC's activities, members, and business address.

2. **Updating Member Information**: Annual reports often include updates on changes in membership, such as the addition or departure of members. Keeping member information current is crucial for accurate legal and financial records.

3. **Financial Information:** Some states may require disclosure of financial information in annual reports. This may include the LLC's gross income, assets, and other financial details. Transparent reporting contributes to accountability and compliance.

4. **Due Dates and Penalties:** It's essential to be aware of the due dates for filing annual reports, as missing deadlines can result in penalties, late fees, or even administrative dissolution of the LLC. Staying organized and setting reminders helps ensure timely submissions.

Record-Keeping:

1. **Legal Compliance:** Comprehensive record-keeping is crucial for demonstrating legal compliance. Maintaining records related to the formation of the LLC, Articles of Organization, operating agreements, and other legal documents provides a historical record of the business's journey.

2. **Financial Records:** Detailed financial records, including income statements, balance sheets, and expense reports, are essential for tax compliance, financial planning, and decision-making. These records support accurate and timely filing of tax returns.

3. **Employee Records:** If the LLC has employees, meticulous record-keeping of employment-related information is essential.

This includes records of hiring, employment contracts, performance evaluations, and any disciplinary actions.

4. **Contracts and Agreements:** Keep copies of all contracts, agreements, and legal documents entered into by the LLC. This includes contracts with vendors, clients, and partners. Thorough documentation helps prevent misunderstandings and disputes.

5. **Meeting Minutes:** Documenting minutes of meetings, especially those involving major business decisions, is a good governance practice. This provides evidence of compliance with legal requirements and ensures transparency among members.

6. **Tax Records:** Retain all tax-related documents, including receipts, invoices, and supporting documentation for deductions. Tax records should be kept for the duration required by tax authorities, which is typically several years.

7. **Licenses and Permits:** Keep records of all business licenses, permits, and regulatory

approvals. This documentation is vital for demonstrating compliance with local, state, and federal regulations.

Digital Record-Keeping:

1. **Secure Storage**: In today's digital age, secure digital storage of records is becoming increasingly common. Cloud-based platforms and secure servers provide convenient and accessible options for storing electronic records.

2. **Backup and Redundancy:** Implement robust backup and redundancy measures to protect digital records from loss or corruption. Regularly back up critical data and consider having redundant storage solutions.

3. **Data Security:** Prioritize data security to protect sensitive information. Implement encryption, password protection, and other security measures to safeguard electronic records from unauthorized access.

Review and Audits:

1. **Regular Review:** Conduct regular reviews of records to ensure accuracy, completeness, and compliance. This proactive approach helps identify any discrepancies or issues that may require correction.

2. **Internal and External Audits:** Consider internal audits or engage external auditors to review the LLC's records and processes. Audits can uncover areas for improvement, enhance internal controls, and ensure adherence to legal and regulatory requirements.

Legal Consultation:

1. **Legal Guidance:** When in doubt about record-keeping requirements or compliance issues, seek legal guidance. Legal professionals can provide specific advice tailored to the business's industry, location, and unique circumstances.

2. **Adaptation to Changes:** Periodically review and update record-keeping practices to adapt to changes in the business environment, regulatory landscape, and technological advancements.

This ensures that record-keeping remains effective and relevant over time.

By prioritizing annual reporting and meticulous record-keeping, LLCs can establish a foundation of transparency, accountability, and compliance. These practices not only fulfill legal obligations but also contribute to the overall efficiency and resilience of the business. As the business landscape evolves, maintaining robust record-keeping processes becomes increasingly valuable for long-term success.

Chapter 5

Managing Finances and Accounting for Your LLC

Effectively managing finances and maintaining accurate accounting records are paramount for the success and sustainability of any business, including Limited Liability Companies (LLCs). In this chapter, we will delve into the essential aspects of managing finances for an LLC, covering the setup of business accounts, basic accounting principles, and the importance of budgeting and financial management.

5.1 Setting Up Business Accounts

Establishing dedicated business accounts is a foundational step in financial management for an LLC. It not only promotes clarity in financial transactions but also enhances professionalism and facilitates compliance with legal and tax obligations. Let's explore the key considerations for setting up business accounts.

Separation of Personal and Business Finances:

1. **Business Checking Account:** Open a separate business checking account for your LLC. This account should be used exclusively for business-related transactions, such as receiving income, making purchases, and paying expenses. A dedicated business account helps maintain a clear separation between personal and business finances.

2. **Business Savings Account**: Consider opening a business savings account to set aside funds for future expenses, emergencies, or growth initiatives. A savings account can also serve as a buffer for unexpected fluctuations in cash flow.

3. **Credit Card:** Obtain a business credit card for the LLC. A business credit card simplifies expense tracking, provides a line of credit for necessary purchases, and can contribute to building the business's credit history.

Choosing the Right Financial Institution:

1. **Research and Compare:** Research different financial institutions to find one that aligns with the needs of your LLC. Compare fees, account features, and additional services offered by various banks or credit unions.

2. **Online Banking**: Consider using a bank that offers robust online banking services. Online banking provides convenient access to account information, facilitates electronic transactions, and streamlines financial management.

3. **Business-Friendly Services:** Look for financial institutions that cater specifically to businesses. Some banks offer business-specific services, such as merchant services, payroll processing, and business loans.

Legal and Compliance Considerations:

1. **Compliance with Regulations:** Ensure that the chosen financial institution complies with all legal and regulatory requirements for

business accounts. This is crucial for avoiding potential issues and maintaining good standing.

2. **Obtaining an Employer Identification Number (EIN):** Before opening business accounts, obtain an Employer Identification Number (EIN) from the IRS. An EIN is necessary for tax purposes, opening a business bank account, and hiring employees.

3. **Business Structure Documentation:** Bring the necessary documentation to the bank, including the Articles of Organization, Operating Agreement, and any other legal documents related to the formation of the LLC. Different banks may have varying requirements.

Record-Keeping Practices:

1. **Account Reconciliation:** Regularly reconcile business accounts to ensure accuracy and identify any discrepancies. This involves matching transactions in your accounting records with those in your bank statements.

2. **Digital Documentation:** Embrace digital documentation for financial transactions. Keep

digital records of invoices, receipts, and transaction confirmations. This practice not only reduces paper clutter but also facilitates efficient record-keeping.

3. **Account Access Control:** Implement access controls for business accounts. Limit access to authorized individuals within the LLC to enhance security and prevent unauthorized transactions.

4. **Integration with Accounting Software:** Explore options for integrating your business accounts with accounting software. Many financial institutions offer seamless integration, streamlining the process of recording and categorizing transactions.

Setting up dedicated business accounts establishes a solid financial infrastructure for your LLC. It promotes transparency, simplifies financial management, and positions the business for compliance with legal and regulatory requirements.

5.2 Basic Accounting Principles for LLCs

Sound accounting practices are the backbone of financial management for any business. Understanding basic accounting principles is essential for maintaining accurate records, making informed business decisions, and fulfilling tax obligations. Let's explore the fundamental accounting principles relevant to LLCs.

Accrual vs. Cash Accounting:

1. **Accrual Accounting:** Accrual accounting recognizes revenue and expenses when they are earned or incurred, regardless of when the cash is received or paid. This method provides a more comprehensive view of the business's financial performance over a specific period.

2. **Cash Accounting:** Cash accounting records revenue and expenses only when actual cash transactions occur. It provides a real-time view of the cash flow but may not capture the full financial picture, especially for businesses with delayed payments or prepaid expenses.

Double-Entry Accounting:

1. **Debits and Credits:** Double-entry accounting involves recording each financial transaction with both a debit and a credit. Debits and credits must always balance, ensuring the accuracy of financial records.

2. **Assets, Liabilities, and Equity:** Transactions are categorized into three main types: assets (what the business owns), liabilities (what the business owes), and equity (the owners' interest in the business). Every transaction affects at least two accounts, maintaining the accounting equation: Assets = Liabilities + Equity.

Chart of Accounts:

1. **Organized Categories:** The chart of accounts is a structured list of all the accounts used by the business. It organizes accounts into categories such as assets, liabilities, equity, revenue, and expenses. A well-organized chart of accounts simplifies financial reporting and analysis.

2. **Customization for Specific Needs:** Customize the chart of accounts to suit the

specific needs and structure of your LLC. Tailoring the chart of accounts ensures that financial reports provide relevant and meaningful insights.

Financial Statements:

1. **Balance Sheet:** The balance sheet provides a snapshot of the LLC's financial position at a specific point in time. It lists assets, liabilities, and equity, showcasing the business's net worth.

2. **Income Statement:** Also known as the profit and loss statement, the income statement summarizes revenue, expenses, and profits or losses over a specific period. It provides insights into the business's operational performance.

3. **Cash Flow Statement**: The cash flow statement details the inflow and outflow of cash over a period. It categorizes cash flows into operating, investing, and financing activities, offering a comprehensive view of the business's liquidity.

Recording Transactions:

1. **Journal Entries:** Journal entries are the basic building blocks of accounting. Each transaction is recorded in a journal, documenting the date, accounts affected, and the corresponding amounts. Journal entries are then transferred to the general ledger.

2. **General Ledger:** The general ledger is the central repository of all accounts and their balances. It provides a comprehensive record of financial transactions and is used to prepare financial statements.

Accounting Software:

1. **Efficiency and Accuracy:** Consider using accounting software to streamline record-keeping and financial reporting. Accounting software automates many processes, reducing the likelihood of errors and providing real-time insights into the business's financial health.

2. **Integration with Other Systems:** Look for accounting software that integrates seamlessly with other business systems, such as banking,

invoicing, and inventory management. Integration enhances efficiency and data accuracy.

Financial Analysis:

1. **Ratio Analysis:** Financial ratios provide valuable insights into the financial health and performance of the business. Common ratios include liquidity ratios, profitability ratios, and solvency ratios. Regularly analyzing these ratios aids in decision-making and strategic planning.

2. **Trend Analysis:** Periodically analyze trends in financial statements to identify patterns and deviations. Trend analysis helps in forecasting, budgeting, and making informed decisions for the future.

Professional Assistance:

1. **Accounting Professionals:** Engage the services of accounting professionals if needed. Accountants can provide expertise in complex accounting matters, tax planning, and ensuring compliance with accounting standards.

2. **Regular Audits**: Consider conducting regular internal audits or engaging external auditors to review financial records. Audits enhance accountability, identify areas for improvement, and instill confidence in stakeholders.

Understanding and applying these basic accounting principles is foundational for maintaining accurate financial records and making informed business decisions. By implementing sound accounting practices, your LLC can navigate financial complexities with confidence and contribute to long-term success.

5.3 Budgeting and Financial Management

Budgeting is a strategic tool that empowers LLCs to plan, allocate resources, and achieve financial goals. Effective financial management, supported by a well-structured budget, is instrumental in guiding the business toward profitability and sustainability. Let's explore the importance of budgeting and key principles of financial management for LLCs.

Purpose and Importance of Budgeting:

1. **Strategic Planning:** Budgeting serves as a roadmap for the financial future of the LLC. It involves setting financial goals, allocating resources, and outlining the financial strategies needed to achieve those goals.

2. **Resource Allocation:** A budget helps in allocating resources efficiently. By estimating income and expenses, an LLC can determine how much capital is available for various activities, such as marketing, expansion, and operational improvements.

3. **Performance Evaluation:** Comparing actual financial results with budgeted figures allows for performance evaluation. Variances between budgeted and actual outcomes provide insights into the effectiveness of financial strategies and operational efficiency.

4. **Decision-Making:** Budgets facilitate informed decision-making. When faced with choices regarding expenditures, investments, or pricing strategies, referring to the budget helps ensure that decisions align with the overall financial plan.

Components of a Budget:

1. **Revenue Forecast:** Estimate expected revenue based on sales projections, market trends, and historical data. Consider different revenue streams and factors that may impact sales.

2. **Expense Categories:** Categorize expenses into fixed and variable costs. Fixed costs, such as rent and salaries, remain constant, while variable costs, such as utilities and raw materials, fluctuate based on business activities.

3. **Capital Expenditures:** Include planned investments in capital assets, such as equipment, technology, or facility upgrades. Capital expenditures are crucial for long-term growth and operational efficiency.

4. **Contingency and Emergency Funds:** Allocate funds for unforeseen expenses or emergencies. Having contingency reserves

provides financial flexibility and safeguards against unexpected challenges.

Principles of Financial Management:

1. **Cash Flow Management**: Prioritize effective cash flow management to ensure that the LLC has enough liquidity to cover operational needs. Monitor receivables, payables, and inventory turnover to optimize cash flow.

2. **Risk Management**: Identify and assess potential financial risks. This includes market risks, credit risks, and operational risks. Develop strategies to mitigate risks and ensure the financial stability of the LLC.

3. **Debt Management**: If the LLC utilizes debt financing, manage debt responsibly. Evaluate interest rates, repayment terms, and the impact of debt on overall financial health. Strive to maintain a healthy debt-to-equity ratio.

4. **Profitability Analysis:** Regularly analyze profitability by assessing gross profit margins,

net profit margins, and return on investment. This analysis helps identify areas for improvement and informs pricing strategies.

5. **Working Capital Management:** Effectively manage working capital by optimizing the balance between current assets and liabilities. This involves monitoring inventory levels, receivables, and payables to maintain efficient operations.

Budget Monitoring and Adjustments:

1. **Regular Monitoring:** Actively monitor actual financial performance against budgeted figures. Regularly review income statements, cash flow statements, and balance sheets to identify any discrepancies or variances.

2. **Flexibility and Adaptability:** Budgets should be flexible and adaptable to changing circumstances. If unexpected events or market shifts occur, be prepared to adjust the budget accordingly to reflect the new reality.

3. **Quarterly and Annual Reviews:** Conduct quarterly and annual reviews of the budget. Use

these reviews as opportunities to assess the effectiveness of financial strategies, make adjustments, and set new goals for the upcoming period.

Communication and Collaboration:

1. **Team Involvement:** Involve relevant team members in the budgeting process. Collaborate with department heads, managers, and key stakeholders to gather input and ensure that the budget aligns with the overall objectives of the LLC.

2. **Communication of Financial Goals:** Clearly communicate financial goals and performance expectations to the entire team. Transparency fosters a shared understanding of the business's financial health and encourages collective efforts toward achieving goals.

Investment and Growth Strategies:

1. **Strategic Investments:** Consider strategic investments that align with the business's long-term goals. This may include expanding product lines, entering new markets, or

investing in technology to enhance operational efficiency.

2. **Diversification**: Explore opportunities for diversification to mitigate risks. Diversifying revenue streams, customer bases, or product offerings can enhance the resilience of the LLC in a dynamic business environment.

Professional Guidance:

1. **Financial Advisors:** Seek the guidance of financial advisors for strategic financial planning. Financial advisors can provide insights, market analysis, and recommendations that align with the financial goals of the LLC.

2. **Legal and Tax Professionals:** Engage legal and tax professionals to ensure that financial strategies comply with legal and regulatory requirements. Professionals can also provide guidance on tax planning and optimization.

By embracing budgeting and adhering to sound financial management principles, an LLC can navigate the complexities of the business landscape with confidence. These practices contribute not only to financial stability but also to the strategic growth and long-term success of the business.

Chapter 6

Protecting Your LLC and Managing Risks

In the dynamic landscape of business, safeguarding your Limited Liability Company (LLC) against potential risks is paramount for long-term success. This chapter delves into the critical aspects of protecting your LLC, emphasizing the importance of liability protection, exploring insurance options tailored for LLCs, and providing insights into mitigating legal risks.

6.1 Importance of Liability Protection

The cornerstone of the LLC structure is the invaluable benefit of limited liability protection. Understanding and appreciating the importance of this protection is crucial for every entrepreneur navigating the intricate world of business.

Personal Asset Protection:

One of the primary reasons entrepreneurs opt for an LLC is to shield their personal assets from the liabilities of the business. In the event of financial challenges, debts, or legal disputes, the personal wealth of LLC members remains separate from the company's obligations. This separation ensures that personal savings, homes, and other assets are not at risk.

Reduced Personal Risk:

The limited liability protection of an LLC extends beyond financial matters. In cases of legal disputes or unforeseen events, members are protected from personal responsibility. This reduced personal risk is a fundamental advantage, providing a level of comfort and security as you navigate the complexities of entrepreneurship.

Enhanced Professionalism:

Opting for an LLC not only offers legal protection but also enhances the professionalism of your business. Clients, customers, and business partners often perceive an LLC as a more established and credible entity. This professional image can contribute to building trust and credibility in the marketplace.

LLC BEGINNERS GUIDE 73

Attracting Investors:
For those seeking external investments to fuel business growth, the limited liability structure can be a crucial factor. Investors are more inclined to engage with businesses that minimize personal liability, creating a conducive environment for financial support and partnerships.

Peace of Mind for Entrepreneurial Ventures:
Entrepreneurship inherently involves risk, and while calculated risks drive innovation and growth, protecting yourself from unnecessary exposure is wise. The limited liability structure provides peace of mind, allowing you to focus on strategic business decisions without constant concern about personal financial repercussions.

In essence, the importance of liability protection in an LLC cannot be overstated. It forms the bedrock of a secure and resilient business structure, enabling entrepreneurs to pursue their ventures with confidence and strategic foresight.

6.2 Insurance Options for LLCs

While the limited liability structure of an LLC provides a robust foundation for protection, prudent entrepreneurs recognize the need for additional risk management through insurance. Let's explore the various insurance options tailored for LLCs, enhancing the overall resilience of your business.

General Liability Insurance:
General liability insurance is a fundamental coverage that protects your LLC from common risks such as property damage, bodily injury, and advertising injury. It provides financial assistance in the event of lawsuits, covering legal fees, settlements, and medical expenses. This insurance is particularly crucial for businesses that interact with the public, clients, or operate in physical spaces.

Professional Liability Insurance (Errors and Omissions Insurance):
For businesses offering professional services, professional liability insurance, also known as errors and omissions (E&O) insurance, is essential. It safeguards your LLC against claims of negligence, errors, or omissions in the

services provided. This coverage is particularly relevant for consulting firms, legal practices, and other service-oriented businesses.

Property Insurance:
Protecting the physical assets of your LLC is vital. Property insurance covers losses or damages to buildings, equipment, inventory, and other tangible assets. Whether you operate from a dedicated office space or work remotely, having property insurance ensures that unexpected events such as fire, theft, or natural disasters do not cripple your business.

Workers' Compensation Insurance:
If your LLC has employees, workers' compensation insurance is typically mandatory. It provides coverage for medical expenses and lost wages in the event of work-related injuries or illnesses. This insurance not only fulfills legal requirements but also demonstrates your commitment to the well-being of your workforce.

Cyber Liability Insurance:
In the digital age, protecting your business from cyber threats is paramount. Cyber liability

insurance covers expenses related to data breaches, hacking incidents, and other cyber risks. As businesses increasingly rely on digital infrastructure, this type of insurance is becoming indispensable to safeguard sensitive information and maintain client trust.

Umbrella Insurance:

Umbrella insurance provides an additional layer of protection beyond the limits of your primary liability policies. It is particularly beneficial for businesses facing higher liability risks or those seeking extra peace of mind. Umbrella insurance can be customized to cover various liability scenarios, offering comprehensive protection for your LLC.

Key Person Insurance:

For businesses heavily reliant on key individuals, key person insurance ensures financial stability in the event of the death or disability of a crucial team member. This coverage provides a financial cushion to navigate the potential challenges associated with the loss of key personnel.

Directors and Officers (D&O) Insurance:
If your LLC has a board of directors or officers, D&O insurance protects these individuals from personal losses in the event of legal actions related to management decisions. It is a crucial component for attracting and retaining top talent to contribute to the strategic direction of your business.

Understanding Policy Limits and Deductibles:
When selecting insurance coverage, it's essential to carefully understand policy limits and deductibles. Policy limits represent the maximum amount an insurance company will pay for a covered loss, and deductibles are the out-of-pocket amounts the insured must pay before coverage kicks in. Striking the right balance between adequate coverage and manageable deductibles is key to optimizing your risk management strategy.

Incorporating a comprehensive insurance strategy into your risk management framework fortifies the protection provided by the LLC structure. It demonstrates a commitment to responsible business practices and ensures that unforeseen events do not jeopardize the stability and continuity of your venture.

6.3 Mitigating Legal Risks

Navigating the legal landscape is an inherent part of running a business, and proactive measures to mitigate legal risks are essential for the sustained success of your LLC. Let's explore key strategies to safeguard your business from potential legal challenges.

Robust Operating Agreement:

An Operating Agreement is the internal document that outlines the structure, management, and operations of your LLC. Crafting a robust and comprehensive operating agreement is a proactive step in mitigating legal risks. It clarifies the roles and responsibilities of members, establishes decision-making processes, and provides a framework for dispute resolution. A well-drafted operating agreement can prevent misunderstandings and potential conflicts, fostering a harmonious and legally sound business environment.

Compliance with State Regulations:

Staying in compliance with state regulations is fundamental to mitigating legal risks. Familiarize yourself with the specific requirements of the state where your LLC is registered, including annual reporting obligations, tax filing requirements, and any industry-specific regulations. Failure to comply with state regulations can lead to penalties, legal challenges, and potential dissolution of your LLC.

Adherence to Employment Laws:

If your LLC has employees, strict adherence to employment laws is paramount. This includes compliance with wage and hour regulations, anti-discrimination laws, and workplace safety standards. Creating and implementing clear employment policies, conducting regular training sessions, and staying informed about legal updates help mitigate the risk of employment-related lawsuits.

Contractual Clarity:

Clear and well-drafted contracts are essential for mitigating legal risks in business transactions. Whether engaging with clients, vendors, or partners, ensure that contracts explicitly outline terms, deliverables, responsibilities, and dispute resolution mechanisms. Ambiguities in contracts can lead to legal disputes, making clarity a cornerstone of risk mitigation.

Intellectual Property Protection:
Protecting your intellectual property (IP) is vital for businesses in creative or innovative industries. Whether it's trademarks, patents, or copyrights, securing legal protection for your IP assets prevents unauthorized use and potential legal battles. Conduct thorough IP searches, file necessary applications, and enforce your rights to safeguard the unique aspects of your business.

Data Security and Privacy Compliance:
In an era of increasing digitalization, safeguarding customer data is not only ethical but also a legal imperative. Adhering to data security and privacy regulations, such as the General Data Protection Regulation (GDPR) or the Health Insurance Portability and Accountability Act (HIPAA), if applicable, is crucial. Implement robust cybersecurity

measures, educate employees on data protection practices, and ensure compliance with relevant laws to mitigate the risk of data breaches and legal consequences.

Proactive Risk Assessments:
Regularly conduct proactive risk assessments to identify and address potential legal risks. This involves reviewing business operations, contracts, and internal processes to identify areas of vulnerability. By anticipating potential challenges and implementing preventive measures, you can significantly reduce the likelihood of legal issues arising.

Consultation with Legal Professionals:
Engaging legal professionals is a prudent strategy to navigate the complexities of business law. Establish a relationship with an experienced business attorney who can provide guidance on compliance, contracts, and potential legal pitfalls. Legal counsel can be invaluable in addressing challenges before they escalate, ensuring that your business operates within the bounds of the law.

Insurance as a Risk Mitigation Tool:

Beyond providing financial protection, insurance can also serve as a tool for mitigating legal risks. Tailored insurance policies, such as professional liability insurance or directors and officers insurance, can offer a layer of defense in the face of legal challenges. Work closely with insurance professionals to align your coverage with the specific legal risks associated with your industry and business operations.

In conclusion, a comprehensive approach to managing legal risks involves a combination of proactive measures, adherence to regulations, and strategic use of insurance. By integrating these elements into your overall risk management strategy, your LLC can navigate the legal landscape with resilience and confidence, positioning itself for sustained success in the business arena.

This chapter has provided a thorough exploration of the critical aspects of protecting your LLC and managing risks. From the foundational importance of liability protection to the intricacies of insurance options and the proactive measures to mitigate legal risks, each element contributes to a robust risk management framework. As you implement these strategies, you fortify your business against unforeseen challenges and create a resilient foundation for long-term growth and prosperity. In the subsequent chapters, we will delve into the financial aspects of managing an LLC, exploring topics such as budgeting, financial management, and taxation.

Chapter 7

Growing and Scaling Your LLC

Entrepreneurship is a journey of continuous evolution, and as your Limited Liability Company (LLC) gains traction, the natural progression involves growth and scaling. This chapter explores the strategic considerations of expanding your LLC, delving into the pivotal questions of when and how to scale. Additionally, we'll discuss the crucial aspects of hiring employees and effectively delegating responsibilities to foster sustainable growth.

7.1 Expanding Your LLC: When and How

Knowing When to Expand:
Deciding when to expand your LLC is a delicate balance that requires a keen understanding of your market, financial capabilities, and the overall business landscape. Here are key indicators that may signal the opportune moment for expansion:

1. **Stable Profitability:** Ensure that your LLC has achieved consistent profitability over an extended period. Stable financial performance provides a solid foundation for expansion, reducing the risks associated with scaling prematurely.

2. **Market Demand and Trends:** Monitor market trends and demand for your products or services. If there is a growing demand that your current operations cannot meet, expansion may be a strategic move to capture a larger market share.

3. **Capacity Constraints:** Assess whether your current resources, such as production capacity or service capabilities, are reaching their limits. If you find that you're consistently operating at or near full capacity, expansion may be necessary to accommodate increased demand.

4. **Positive Customer Feedback:** Positive customer feedback and increasing customer loyalty are strong indicators that your business is ready for expansion. Satisfied customers not only contribute to your current success but also serve as advocates for your brand as you grow.

5. **Competitive Landscape:** Evaluate your position in the competitive landscape. If you identify opportunities to gain a competitive advantage through expansion, such as reaching untapped markets or introducing innovative products, it may be the right time to scale.

Strategies for Sustainable Growth:
Once you've identified the opportune moment for expansion, implementing a strategic growth plan is essential for sustainable success. Consider the following strategies as you embark on the journey of growing your LLC:

1. **Market Research and Analysis**: Conduct thorough market research to identify new opportunities and potential challenges. Understand the needs and preferences of your target audience, analyze competitor strategies, and gather insights that will inform your expansion plan.

2. **Diversification of Products or Services:** Explore opportunities to diversify your offerings. Introducing new products or services can broaden your customer base and enhance

your revenue streams. However, ensure that the diversification aligns with your brand and core competencies.

3. **Geographical Expansion**: Consider expanding into new geographic locations. Whether it's entering new cities, regions, or even international markets, geographic expansion allows you to tap into a broader customer base and reduce dependency on a single market.

4. **Strategic Partnerships and Alliances:** Forming strategic partnerships and alliances can be a powerful strategy for growth. Collaborating with complementary businesses or industry leaders can open doors to new opportunities, resources, and customer bases.

5. **Investment in Marketing and Branding**: Increase your investment in marketing and branding efforts to raise awareness of your expanded offerings. Utilize digital marketing, social media, and other channels to reach a wider audience and solidify your position in the market.

6. **Technology Adoption**: Embrace technological advancements to streamline operations and enhance efficiency. Technology can play a pivotal role in scaling your business, whether through improved automation, data analytics, or the implementation of e-commerce solutions.

7. **Customer Retention and Satisfaction**: While focusing on growth, do not overlook the importance of customer retention. Satisfied customers are more likely to become repeat buyers and advocates for your brand, contributing to sustained growth over the long term.

8. **Financial Planning and Funding:** Develop a comprehensive financial plan that accounts for the costs associated with expansion. Whether it's hiring new staff, acquiring additional resources, or investing in marketing, having a clear financial roadmap is crucial. Explore funding options, including loans, investors, or reinvested profits, to support your expansion initiatives.

9. **Scalable Infrastructure:** Ensure that your business infrastructure, including technology, operations, and human resources, is scalable. A flexible and scalable infrastructure allows your business to adapt to increased demands without compromising efficiency or quality.

Common Challenges and Mitigation Strategies:
Despite the potential rewards, expansion comes with its share of challenges. It's essential to anticipate and address these challenges to ensure a smooth growth trajectory:

1. **Financial Strain:** Expansion often requires a significant financial investment. To mitigate financial strain, conduct a thorough cost-benefit analysis, explore financing options, and prioritize initiatives that offer the highest return on investment.

2. **Human Resource Management:** Hiring and managing a growing team can be challenging. Implement effective human resource management practices, invest in employee training, and foster a positive company culture to attract and retain top talent.

3. **Operational Efficiency:** Maintaining operational efficiency during expansion is critical. Streamline processes, invest in technology that enhances efficiency, and regularly assess and optimize your operations to adapt to the increased scale.

4. **Market Saturation:** Before expanding into new markets, carefully assess the level of competition and potential saturation. Differentiate your offerings, tailor your marketing strategies, and identify unique selling points to stand out in competitive environments.

5. **Customer Service Excellence:** As your customer base expands, maintaining high levels of customer service becomes paramount. Invest in customer support systems, gather feedback, and continuously improve your service to ensure customer satisfaction.

6. **Adaptability to Change:** The business landscape is dynamic, and adaptability is key to successful expansion. Stay agile, monitor market trends, and be prepared to adjust your strategies based on changing conditions.

By strategically approaching expansion and addressing potential challenges, your LLC can navigate the complexities of growth with resilience and precision. This not only positions your business for success but also establishes a foundation for sustainable long-term growth.

7.2 Hiring Employees and Delegating Responsibilities

As your LLC expands, the role of effective delegation and strategic hiring becomes paramount. Building a capable and motivated team is instrumental in realizing your growth objectives. Let's explore the intricacies of hiring employees and delegating responsibilities to foster a culture of collaboration and efficiency.

Strategic Hiring:

1. **Identifying Talent Needs**: Conduct a thorough assessment of your current team and identify areas where additional talent is needed. Consider the skills, expertise, and experience required to support your growth initiatives.

2. **Creating Detailed Job Descriptions**: Craft detailed and accurate job descriptions for open positions. Clearly outline responsibilities, qualifications, and expectations to attract candidates who align with your organizational needs.

3. **Recruitment Strategies:** Implement effective recruitment strategies to attract top talent. Utilize online job platforms, professional networks, and referrals to reach a diverse pool of candidates. Leverage social media and employer branding to showcase your company culture and values.

4. **Interview and Selection Process**: Develop a comprehensive interview and selection process to assess candidates thoroughly. Consider incorporating multiple interview rounds, skills assessments, and team interviews to evaluate both technical abilities and cultural fit.

5. **Onboarding and Training:** Once you've hired new team members, prioritize a robust onboarding and training process. This ensures that employees are equipped with the necessary

knowledge and resources to contribute effectively from day one.

6. **Employee Retention Strategies**: In a competitive job market, retaining top talent is as important as hiring them. Implement employee retention strategies, such as professional development opportunities, a positive work environment, and competitive compensation packages.

Effective Delegation:

1. **Understanding Your Team:** Before delegating responsibilities, understand the strengths, skills, and preferences of your team members. This knowledge allows you to assign tasks that align with each individual's capabilities and interests.

2. **Setting Clear Expectations:** Clearly communicate expectations when delegating tasks. Define the scope of the assignment, desired outcomes, and any specific guidelines or deadlines. This clarity minimizes misunderstandings and ensures that team

members have a clear understanding of their responsibilities.

3. **Empowering Team Members:** Empower your team by providing them with the autonomy to make decisions within their designated responsibilities. This fosters a sense of ownership and accountability, motivating team members to excel in their roles.

4. **Effective Communication:** Establish open and transparent communication channels within your team. Encourage regular updates, feedback sessions, and collaborative discussions to ensure everyone is aligned with organizational goals and objectives.

5. **Building a Culture of Trust:** Trust is a foundational element of effective delegation. Build a culture of trust within your team by demonstrating confidence in your team members' abilities and providing constructive feedback. Trust encourages a collaborative and positive work environment.

6. **Monitoring Progress and Providing Support:** While delegating tasks, maintain a

proactive approach to monitoring progress. Regularly check in with team members, offer support when needed, and celebrate achievements. Address any challenges promptly to prevent issues from escalating.

7. Encouraging Professional Development:
Foster a culture of continuous learning and professional development. Provide opportunities for skill enhancement, training programs, and mentorship to empower your team members to grow within their roles.

8. Delegating Leadership Responsibilities: As your team expands, consider delegating leadership responsibilities to capable individuals within the organization. Empowering leaders within different departments or teams contributes to a decentralized leadership structure, fostering efficiency and innovation.

Challenges of Delegation and Hiring:
While hiring employees and delegating responsibilities are essential components of growth, they come with their own set of challenges. Addressing these challenges

proactively ensures a smooth transition into a larger and more complex organizational structure:

1. **Finding the Right Fit:** Identifying candidates who not only possess the required skills but also align with your company culture can be challenging. Invest time in the recruitment process to ensure a strong fit with your team dynamics.

2. **Balancing Autonomy and Oversight:** Striking the right balance between empowering team members with autonomy and providing necessary oversight can be delicate. Regular communication and a clear framework for accountability help navigate this challenge.

3. **Ensuring Consistent Quality:** Maintaining consistent quality as your team expands is crucial. Implementing standardized processes, quality control measures, and ongoing training programs contribute to maintaining high standards.

4. **Managing Team Dynamics:** With a growing team, managing interpersonal dynamics

becomes more complex. Proactively address conflicts, encourage open communication, and foster a positive team culture to mitigate potential challenges.

5. **Adapting Leadership Style:** As your team grows, your leadership style may need to adapt. Being flexible and responsive to the evolving needs of your team is essential for effective leadership in a changing organizational landscape.

By strategically navigating the hiring process and mastering the art of delegation, your LLC can build a resilient and dynamic team that fuels sustainable growth. The synergy of talented individuals working collaboratively under effective leadership positions your business for success in the competitive marketplace.

In conclusion, Chapter 7 has provided a comprehensive exploration of the strategic considerations involved in growing and scaling your LLC. From recognizing the opportune moment for expansion to implementing effective hiring practices and mastering the art of delegation, each aspect contributes to building a resilient and agile organization. As you apply these insights to your business, you lay the groundwork for sustained success and a thriving future. In the subsequent chapters, we will delve into the financial aspects of managing an expanding LLC, exploring topics such as budgeting, financial management, and taxation in the context of growth and scalability.

Chapter 8

Financial Management for Growing LLCs

As your Limited Liability Company (LLC) experiences growth and expansion, the dynamics of financial management become increasingly intricate. This chapter delves into the core aspects of financial management for growing LLCs, addressing the strategic importance of budgeting for expansion, the nuances of effective cash flow management, and the challenges and considerations surrounding taxation during the growth phase.

8.1 Budgeting for Expansion: Strategic Financial Planning

Budgeting for expansion is a linchpin in the financial success and sustainability of a growing LLC. Strategic financial planning not only guides your day-to-day operations but also lays the groundwork for robust decision-making and resource allocation. Let's explore key considerations and actionable steps in budgeting for expansion:

Understanding Growth Objectives:

1. **Define Clear Objectives:** Clearly articulate your growth objectives. Whether it's entering new markets, expanding product lines, or increasing market share, having well-defined goals provides a roadmap for your budgeting process.

2. **Assess Resource Requirements:** Evaluate the resources needed to achieve your growth objectives. This includes human resources, technology, marketing, and operational infrastructure. A comprehensive understanding of resource requirements informs your budget allocations.

3. **Anticipate Capital Expenditures:** As you plan for expansion, anticipate any capital expenditures required. This may include investments in equipment, technology upgrades, or physical expansion. Accurate forecasting of capital expenditures prevents financial surprises during the expansion phase.

Developing a Comprehensive Budget:

1. **Revenue Projections:** Develop realistic revenue projections based on market analysis, historical performance, and growth forecasts. Consider factors such as pricing strategy, market demand, and potential challenges.

2. **Operating Expenses:** Review and update your operating expenses. As your LLC grows, operating expenses may evolve, requiring adjustments in areas such as marketing, staffing, and overhead costs. Ensure that your budget reflects the current and anticipated needs of your expanding operations.

3. **Working Capital Requirements:** Analyze working capital requirements to sustain day-to-day operations. Adequate working capital is essential for managing short-term obligations, fulfilling customer orders, and navigating fluctuations in cash flow.

4. **Contingency Planning:** Incorporate contingency planning into your budget. Unforeseen challenges or opportunities may arise during expansion, and having a

contingency fund provides financial flexibility and resilience.

5. Investment in Marketing and Branding: Allocate a substantial portion of your budget to marketing and branding initiatives. Effectively promoting your expanded offerings and reaching new audiences is integral to the success of your growth strategy.

Monitoring and Adjusting the Budget:

1. Regular Monitoring: Implement a system for regular monitoring of your budget against actual performance. Establish key performance indicators (KPIs) to track progress and identify any deviations from the budgeted plan.

2. Flexibility and Adjustments: Maintain flexibility in your budget to accommodate changes in the business landscape. An agile budgeting approach allows you to adjust allocations based on real-time feedback, market dynamics, and evolving business conditions.

3. Communication and Team Alignment: Foster communication and alignment within your team regarding budgetary goals and constraints. A cohesive understanding of the budget ensures that all team members contribute to financial discipline and accountability.

4. Financial Education for Team Members: Provide financial education and training for relevant team members. Empowering your team with financial literacy enhances their understanding of budgetary considerations and encourages responsible financial behavior.

Utilizing Technology for Budgeting:

1. **Implement Budgeting Software**: Explore the use of budgeting software to streamline the budgeting process. These tools offer features such as real-time tracking, scenario analysis, and collaboration, enhancing the efficiency and accuracy of your budgeting efforts.

2. **Integration with Financial Systems:** Ensure seamless integration between budgeting software and your overall financial systems. This integration allows for a cohesive and synchronized approach to financial

management, from budget creation to performance analysis.

3. **Data-Driven Decision-Making:** Leverage data analytics to inform your budgeting decisions. Analyzing historical data, market trends, and key performance metrics empowers you to make informed and data-driven choices in your budgeting process.

In essence, budgeting for expansion is a dynamic and strategic process that requires a forward-thinking approach. By aligning your budget with growth objectives, continuously monitoring and adjusting based on real-time feedback, and leveraging technology for efficiency, you position your LLC for financial resilience and success during periods of growth.

8.2 Managing Cash Flow Effectively

Effective cash flow management is the lifeblood of any growing LLC. As your business expands, the intricacies of managing cash flow become more pronounced. This section explores the fundamental principles and practical strategies for managing cash flow effectively during periods of growth:

Forecasting Cash Flow:

1. **Accurate Revenue Forecasting**: Develop accurate revenue forecasts based on realistic sales projections. Understanding the timing and volume of incoming cash is crucial for planning expenditures and meeting financial obligations.

2. **Detailed Expense Projections:** Project your expenses with granularity. Consider not only fixed costs but also variable costs associated with increased sales or expanded operations. Detailed expense projections enable you to anticipate cash outflows accurately.

3. **Accounts Receivable Management:** Implement robust accounts receivable management practices. Ensure timely and consistent invoicing, offer incentives for early payments, and establish clear credit terms to accelerate cash collection.

4. **Inventory Optimization**: If your business involves inventory, optimize your inventory management. Balancing inventory levels with

demand prevents excess holding costs and frees up cash for other operational needs.

Strategic Cash Flow Strategies:

1. **Negotiate Favorable Payment Terms:** Negotiate favorable payment terms with suppliers and vendors. Extending payment terms or securing discounts for early payments can positively impact your cash flow position.

2. **Explore Financing Options:** Explore financing options to supplement your cash flow. This may include securing a line of credit, invoice financing, or short-term loans. Evaluate the cost and terms of financing to align with your growth strategy.

3. **Cash Flow Budgeting**: Develop a dedicated cash flow budget to track the movement of cash in and out of your business. A cash flow budget provides a real-time snapshot of your liquidity position and informs proactive decision-making.

4. **Emergency Fund for Contingencies:** Establish an emergency fund to address

unforeseen challenges. Having a financial buffer safeguards your business against unexpected events that may impact cash flow, providing a safety net during periods of uncertainty.

Implementing Cash Flow Technologies:

1. **Automated Invoicing and Payment Systems:** Implement automated invoicing and payment systems to streamline cash flow processes. Automation reduces administrative overhead, accelerates cash collection, and enhances overall efficiency.

2. **Cash Flow Forecasting Tools**: Utilize cash flow forecasting tools to project future cash positions. These tools use historical data, current financial metrics, and predictive algorithms to provide insights into your future cash flow, enabling proactive decision-making.

3. **Integration with Accounting Software:** Ensure seamless integration between cash flow management tools and your accounting software. Integration enhances accuracy and

reduces manual errors, allowing for a cohesive financial management ecosystem.

Building a Cash Reserve:

1. **Prioritizing Cash Reserve:** Prioritize the accumulation of a cash reserve during periods of positive cash flow. A robust cash reserve acts as a financial cushion, providing stability and flexibility during lean periods or unexpected challenges.

2. **Continuous Monitoring and Adjustments:** Continuously monitor your cash flow position and make adjustments as needed. Proactive management of cash flow requires vigilance, regular analysis, and the flexibility to adapt to changing circumstances.

3. **Investing Surplus Cash:** Strategically invest surplus cash to generate additional income. Explore low-risk investment options that align with your risk tolerance and liquidity needs, contributing to the overall financial health of your business.

Effectively managing cash flow is an ongoing process that demands attention to detail, strategic foresight, and the agility to adapt to changing circumstances. By implementing proactive cash flow strategies, utilizing technological tools, and fostering a culture of financial discipline, your growing LLC can navigate the complexities of cash flow management with confidence.

8.3 Navigating Taxation Challenges in the Growth Phase

Navigating taxation challenges is a critical aspect of financial management for any growing LLC. As your business expands, the complexity of tax considerations increases, requiring a strategic and proactive approach to ensure compliance and optimize your tax position. This section addresses key taxation challenges and provides guidance on navigating them effectively:

Understanding Tax Implications:

1. **Impact of Business Structure on Taxation:** Revisit the tax implications of your chosen business structure. Evaluate whether the tax

advantages of an LLC remain optimal as your business grows or if alternative structures may offer more favorable tax treatment.

2. **Assessing Tax Liabilities:** Assess your current and anticipated tax liabilities. Consider factors such as increased revenue, expanded operations, and changes in profitability. An accurate assessment of tax obligations informs your financial planning and resource allocation.

3. **State and Local Tax Considerations**: Be mindful of state and local tax considerations. As your business expands into new regions, understand the tax obligations specific to each jurisdiction. Compliance with state and local tax regulations is integral to avoiding penalties and legal complications.

Strategies for Tax Optimization:

1. **Utilizing Tax Credits and Incentives:** Explore available tax credits and incentives. Many jurisdictions offer credits for specific activities, such as research and development or job creation. Utilizing these incentives can significantly reduce your overall tax burden.

2. **Timing of Expenses and Deductions:** Strategically time your business expenses and deductions. Consider accelerating deductible expenses when beneficial, and explore opportunities to defer income to optimize your taxable income in a given year.

3. **Reviewing Depreciation and Amortization:** Review and optimize depreciation and amortization strategies. Assess whether your current methods align with your growth strategy and whether adjustments can be made to enhance tax efficiency.

4. **Engaging Tax Professionals:** Engage experienced tax professionals. As your business grows, the complexity of tax regulations increases. Collaborating with tax experts ensures that you navigate the nuances of tax laws, identify opportunities for optimization, and remain compliant.

Compliance with Regulatory Changes:

1. **Stay Informed About Tax Law Changes:** Stay informed about changes in tax laws and

regulations. The landscape of taxation is dynamic, with laws evolving at local, national, and international levels. Regularly update your knowledge to ensure compliance and leverage new opportunities.

2. **Proactive Adaptation to Regulatory Changes:** Adopt a proactive approach to adapting to regulatory changes. Anticipate the impact of upcoming tax reforms on your business, and adjust your financial strategies accordingly. Proactivity minimizes the risk of non-compliance and positions your business for success in a changing tax environment.

International Expansion Considerations:

1. **Cross-Border Tax Implications:** If your LLC expands internationally, consider the cross-border tax implications. International taxation involves complex considerations, including transfer pricing, withholding taxes, and compliance with tax treaties. Seek professional advice to navigate the intricacies of global taxation.

2. **Structuring International Operations Tax-Efficiently:** Structure international operations in a tax-efficient manner. Consider establishing entities in jurisdictions with favorable tax regimes, optimizing transfer pricing strategies, and leveraging international tax planning to minimize overall tax liabilities.

Record-Keeping and Documentation:

1. **Maintaining Comprehensive Records:** Maintain comprehensive records of financial transactions, expenses, and income. Accurate record-keeping is essential for both tax compliance and strategic decision-making. Invest in robust accounting systems to streamline record-keeping processes.

2. **Documentation of Deductions and Credits:** Document all eligible deductions and credits. In the event of an audit or tax review, having thorough documentation provides evidence of your eligibility for specific tax incentives, reducing the risk of disputes with tax authorities.

Navigating Audits and Inquiries:

1. **Collaborating with Tax Professionals:** In the event of an audit or inquiry, collaborate closely with tax professionals. Professional representation ensures that you navigate the audit process efficiently, respond to inquiries accurately, and address any issues with the expertise required.

2. **Proactive Compliance Measures:** Adopt proactive compliance measures to minimize the risk of audits. Regularly review your tax filings, adhere to reporting deadlines, and implement internal controls to ensure accuracy and consistency in your financial reporting.

In conclusion, navigating taxation challenges during the growth phase requires a proactive, informed, and strategic approach. By understanding the implications of your business structure, optimizing tax strategies, staying compliant with regulatory changes, and maintaining meticulous record-keeping, your growing LLC can navigate the complexities of taxation with confidence and efficiency.

As you implement these financial management strategies for budgeting, cash flow management, and taxation during the growth phase, remember that each decision contributes to the overall financial health and sustainability of your LLC. The subsequent chapters will further explore financial considerations, including budgeting for specific business functions, optimizing financial performance, and positioning your LLC for long-term success in a competitive market.

Conclusion

Navigating the Journey of Entrepreneurship with Your LLC

As we conclude this comprehensive guide, "LLC Beginners Guide," it's essential to reflect on the multifaceted journey of entrepreneurship and the pivotal role that your Limited Liability Company (LLC) plays in this dynamic landscape. Throughout the preceding chapters, we've delved into the intricacies of forming, managing, and growing an LLC, providing insights, strategies, and practical guidance for both novice entrepreneurs and seasoned business leaders. This concluding chapter aims to distill key takeaways, emphasize the significance of continuous learning, and offer a forward-looking perspective as you navigate the exciting path of business ownership.

Reflecting on the Fundamentals:
The foundation of your entrepreneurial venture lies in the well-thought-out decisions made during the formation of your LLC. Understanding the basics, such as the structure

of an LLC, its advantages and disadvantages, and the key features that distinguish it, sets the stage for a resilient and adaptable business structure. This fundamental understanding empowers you to make informed choices aligned with your business goals, risk tolerance, and vision for the future.

Strategic Decision-Making in LLC Ownership:
Deciding whether an LLC is the right business structure for your venture involves a nuanced evaluation of various factors, from liability protection to tax considerations. The strategic decision-making process outlined in Chapter 2 guides you through considerations such as business nature, liability protection, tax implications, management preferences, and growth aspirations. Recognizing the unique needs of your enterprise enables you to align your LLC ownership with the overarching goals of your business.

Exploring Growth and Scalability:
The journey of entrepreneurship is inherently dynamic, and growth is a natural evolution. Chapter 7 delves into the strategic

considerations of expanding your LLC, emphasizing the critical questions of when and how to scale. The exploration of hiring employees and delegating responsibilities underscores the importance of building a capable and motivated team to support your business's growth trajectory. As you navigate the challenges and opportunities of expansion, the emphasis on effective delegation and strategic hiring serves as a compass for sustainable scalability.

Protecting Your LLC:
Protecting your LLC is not only a legal imperative but a strategic necessity for long-term success. Chapter 6 emphasizes the importance of liability protection, exploring the foundational elements of limited liability that shield your personal assets from business obligations. The discussion on insurance options for LLCs underscores the role of risk management in safeguarding your business. By mitigating legal risks through a robust operating agreement, compliance with state regulations, and proactive measures, you fortify the resilience of your LLC against unforeseen challenges.

Financial Management in the Context of Growth:

The growth of your LLC is intrinsically tied to sound financial management. As you embark on the journey of expansion, effective budgeting, financial planning, and taxation strategies become indispensable. The subsequent chapters in this guide will delve into the intricacies of financial management in the context of growth, providing actionable insights into budgeting for expansion, managing cash flow, and navigating the complexities of taxation.

Continuous Learning and Adaptability:

The entrepreneurial landscape is marked by its fluidity and constant evolution. Embracing a mindset of continuous learning and adaptability is a hallmark of successful entrepreneurs. Whether it's staying abreast of changes in regulations, adopting new technologies, or refining your leadership skills, the ability to adapt positions you as a resilient and forward-thinking business owner.

Looking Ahead:

As you conclude this guide and embark on the ongoing journey of entrepreneurship with your LLC, consider the following key principles:

1. **Strategic Vision:** Maintain a clear and strategic vision for your business. Regularly revisit and refine your business goals, adapting them to the evolving landscape and opportunities that arise.

2. **Adaptability:** Embrace change and be adaptable in the face of challenges. The ability to pivot, innovate, and evolve is a distinguishing trait of successful entrepreneurs.

3. **Investment in People:** Recognize the value of your team and invest in their growth and development. A motivated and skilled team is a cornerstone of sustained success.

4. **Ethical Business Practices**: Uphold ethical business practices and prioritize integrity in all your dealings. Trust and credibility are invaluable assets in the world of entrepreneurship.

5. **Risk Management**: Continuously assess and manage risks. Implement proactive risk mitigation strategies and stay vigilant to emerging threats that may impact your business.

6. **Strategic Partnerships:** Explore strategic partnerships that align with your business objectives. Collaborations can open new avenues for growth and provide valuable resources and expertise.

7. **Customer-Centric Approach:** Maintain a customer-centric approach. Listen to customer feedback, adapt to their needs, and cultivate strong relationships to foster loyalty and brand advocacy.

8. **Community Engagement**: Engage with your local and industry communities. Building strong connections contributes to a supportive network and opens doors to collaboration and opportunities.

In the ever-evolving landscape of entrepreneurship, your LLC serves as both a legal framework and a reflection of your

LLC BEGINNERS GUIDE 122

entrepreneurial spirit. As you navigate the complexities of business ownership, remember that each decision, each challenge, and each triumph contributes to the tapestry of your entrepreneurial journey. By approaching each aspect of your LLC with diligence, strategic foresight, and a commitment to excellence, you position yourself for a fulfilling and prosperous trajectory in the world of business.

As you apply the insights from this guide to your unique entrepreneurial journey, I wish you continued success, growth, and fulfillment in the pursuit of your business goals. The journey of entrepreneurship is a continual adventure, and your LLC is the vessel that propels you toward new horizons. May your path be marked by innovation, resilience, and the realization of your boldest entrepreneurial aspirations.

As we conclude this journey through the intricacies of Limited Liability Companies (LLCs), I extend heartfelt gratitude to you, the reader. Your pursuit of knowledge and commitment to entrepreneurial excellence inspire us. The success of this guide lies in your curiosity, determination, and passion for building and growing businesses. I hope the insights provided have enriched your understanding and equipped you for success in your ventures. Your journey is our shared venture, and your feedback is invaluable. I invite you to leave a review, sharing your thoughts and experiences. May your LLC thrive, and your entrepreneurial spirit continue to shape a future of innovation and prosperity. Thank you for being an integral part of this entrepreneurial community.

About The Author

Mike R. Peterson is a professional entrepreneur renowned for his visionary leadership and innovative business strategies. With a career spanning over two decades, Peterson has made significant contributions to various industries, including technology, finance, and healthcare. Armed with a strong educational background, he earned a degree in business management from a prestigious university before embarking on his entrepreneurial journey.

Peterson's entrepreneurial spirit led him to establish and successfully manage multiple ventures, showcasing his adaptability and resilience in the ever-evolving business landscape. He is widely recognized for his ability to identify emerging trends and capitalize on market opportunities, which has resulted in the sustained success of his enterprises.

Beyond his business acumen, Peterson is known for his commitment to corporate social responsibility, actively engaging in philanthropic endeavors and community development projects. His leadership style emphasizes collaboration, innovation, and a strong commitment to ethical business practices. Mike R. Peterson continues to inspire aspiring entrepreneurs through his achievements, leaving an indelible mark on the business world.